WORKBOOK

2

T0351737

PEARSON

My Little Island 2
Workbook

Pearson Education, 10 Bank Street, White Plains, NY 10606 USA

Staff credits: The people who made up the **My Little Island** team, representing editorial, production, design, manufacturing, and marketing are Rhea Banker, Carol Brown, Tracey Munz Cataldo, Dave Dickey, Gina DiLillo, Christine Edmonds, Nancy Flaggman, Yoko Mia Hirano, Caroline Kasterine, Ed Lamprich, Theodore Lane, Christopher Leonowicz, Emily Lippincott, Maria Pia Marrella, Kate McLoughlin, Linda Moser, Leslie Patterson, Pamela Pia, Donna Schaffer, Mairead Stack, Kenneth Volcjak, and Lauren Weidenman.
Text design: Tracey Munz Cataldo, Maria Pia Marrella
Text composition: TSI Graphics
Text font: Fiendstar Bold
Illustrations: José Luis Briseño

www.pearsonelt.com

ISBN-10: 0-13-279540-X
ISBN-13: 978-0-13-279540-1

Printed in China
23   22

Contents

1 Welcome

1 Trace. Color black or gray and say.

Practice: *black, gray*

SHAPES

2 Trace, color, and say.

Practice: shapes

3 Match. Color and say.

Practice: classroom objects

REVIEW

4 Trace and say. Color.

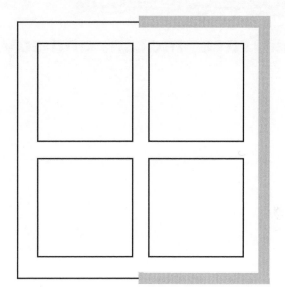

Toys

5 Trace, match, and say. Color.

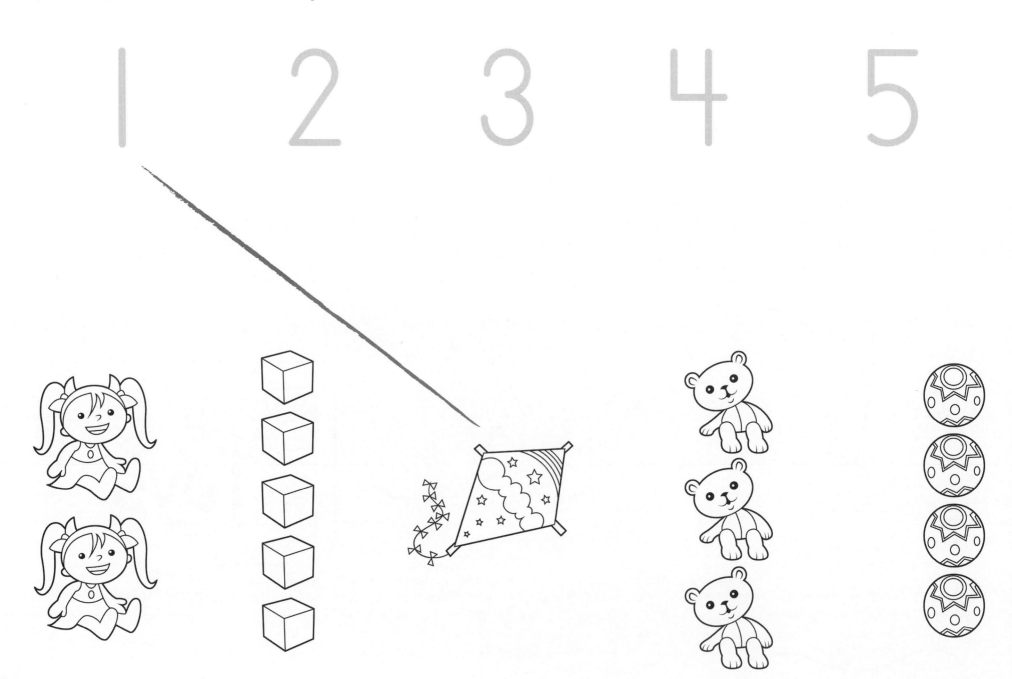

1   2   3   4   5

8

Practice: toys, numbers 1–5

6 **Draw your face. Color and say.**

REVIEW

7 Connect the dots. Color and say.

Practice: family members, food items

REVIEW

8 **Match, color, and say.**

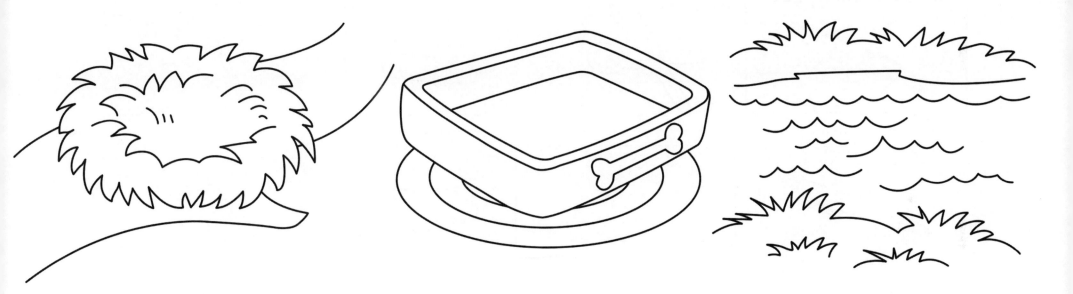

Practice: animals

2 My School

1 What's missing? Draw and say. Color.

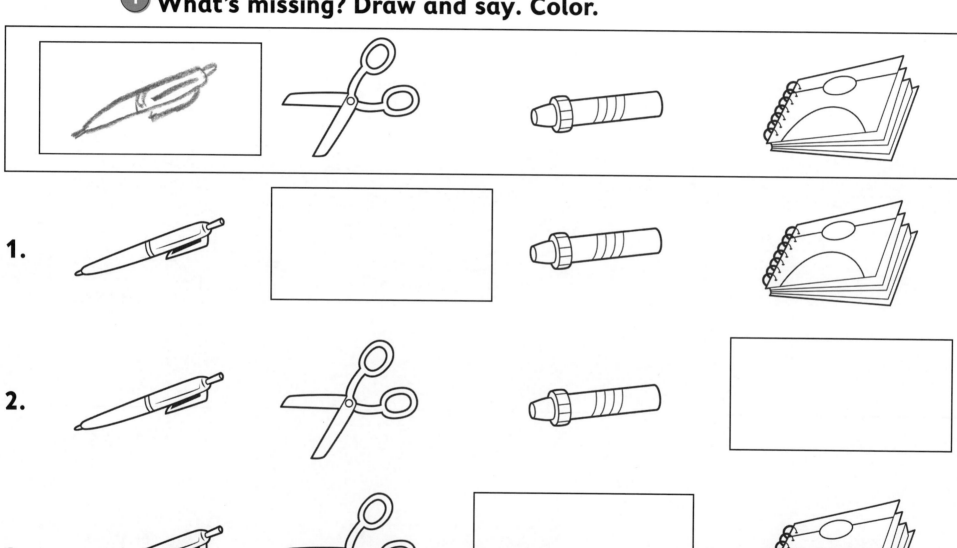

1.

2.

3.

Practice: *marker, notebook, pen, scissors*

STORY

2 **Draw Sammy. Ask and answer. Color.**

Practice: *This is my [computer]. Is it a [backpack]? Yes, it is. / No, it isn't.*

SPEAKING

3 Circle the difference in Box B. Color. Ask and answer.

A   B

Practice: *Is it a [marker]? Yes, it is. / No, it isn't.*

SPEAKING

4 Trace, color, and say. Ask and answer.

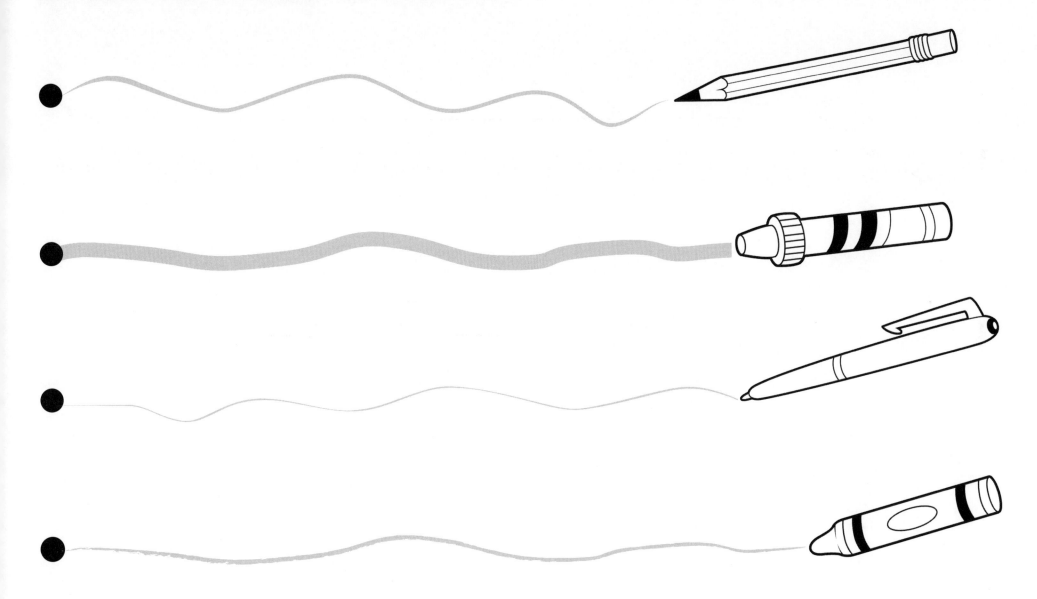

Practice: *Is it a [pencil]? Yes, it is. / No, it isn't.*

5 **Trace, color, and say.**

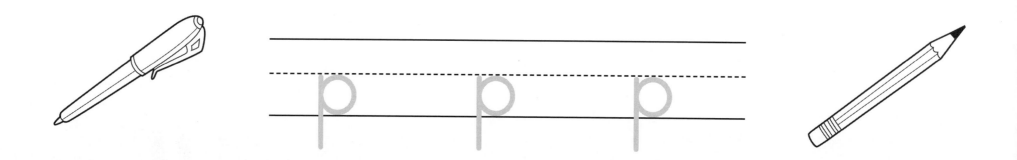

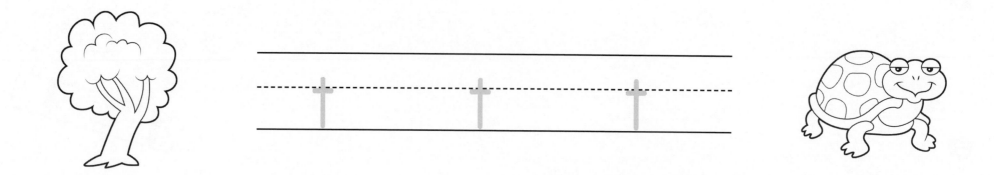

Phonics: initial *p* and *t* sounds **Review:** *pencil, tree, turtle*

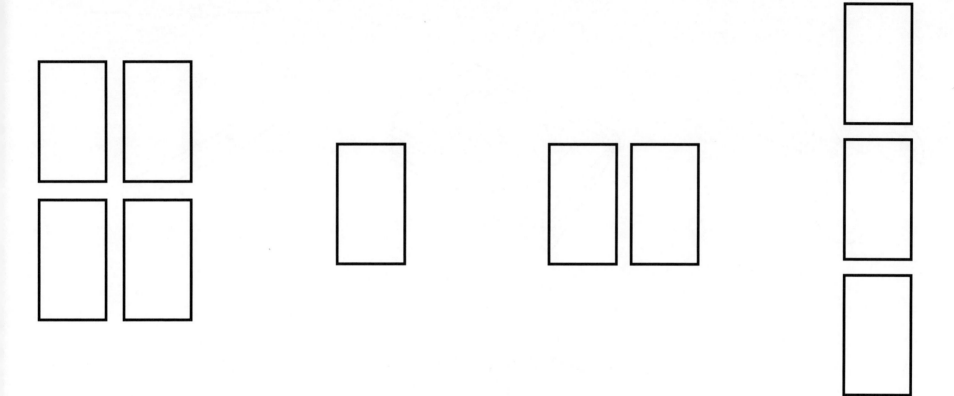

1   2   3   4

7 Match and say. Color.

Put things away.

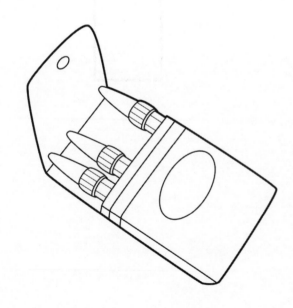

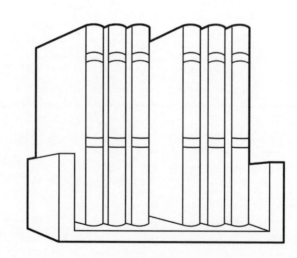

Values: Put [things] away. **Review:** school vocabulary

 **I can!**

8 **Draw 5 items. Color. Ask and answer.**

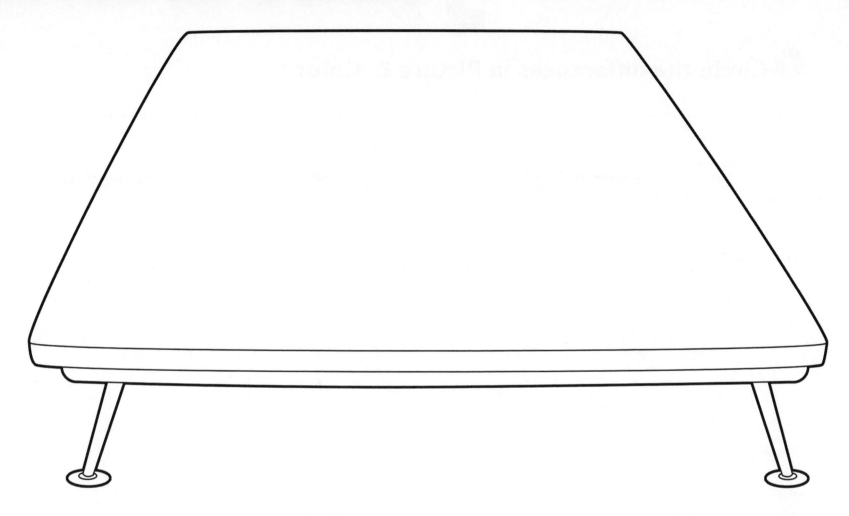

Review: classroom objects; *Is it a [notebook]? Yes, it is. / No, it isn't.*

3 Family

1 Circle the differences in Picture B. Color.

Practice: *brother, cousin, father, mother, pet, sister*

STORY

2 **Color. Ask and answer.**

Practice: *Who's she/he? [She's] my [grandma].*

3 **Ask and answer as Billy. Color.**

Practice: *[She's] my [grandma].*

SPEAKING

4 Find. Ask and answer. Color.

Practice: *Who's [he]? [He's] my [brother].*

5 Trace, color, and say.

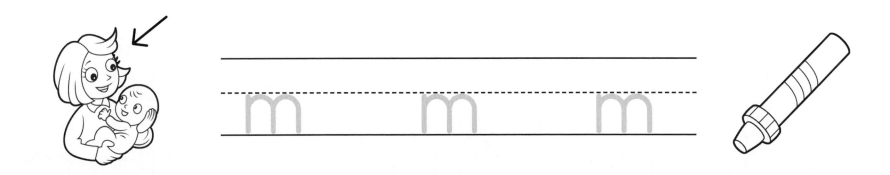

m   m   m

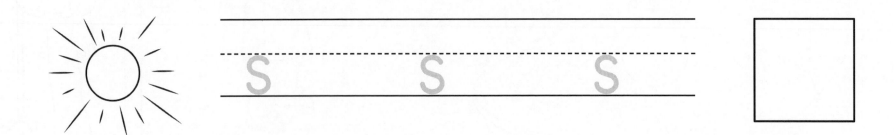

s   s   s

Phonics: initial *m* and *s* sounds **Review:** *mom, square, sun*

SHAPES

6 Trace. Color the stars yellow.

VALUES

7 **Color and say.**

I help.

Values: Help your family. **Review:** family members

REVIEW I can!

8 Draw a family member. Color and say.

Review: family members; *Who's [she]? [She's] my [aunt].*

4 Play Time!

1 Match and say.

Practice: *bike, boat, car, train*

2 Color Billy's toys. Ask and answer.

Practice: *Is it [red]? Yes, it is. / No, it isn't.*

3 **Color. Ask and answer.**

Is it a train?

30

Practice: *Is it a [train]? Yes, it is. / No, it isn't.*

4 **Color. Ask and answer.**

Practice: *Is it [red]? Yes, it is. It's the [car].*

5 Trace, color, and say.

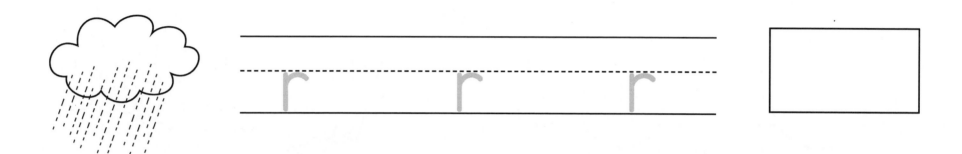

r r r r

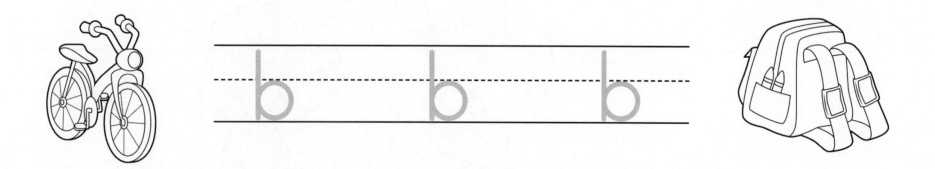

b b b b

Phonics: initial *r* and *b* sounds **Review:** *rain*

6 Trace. Count and say. Color.

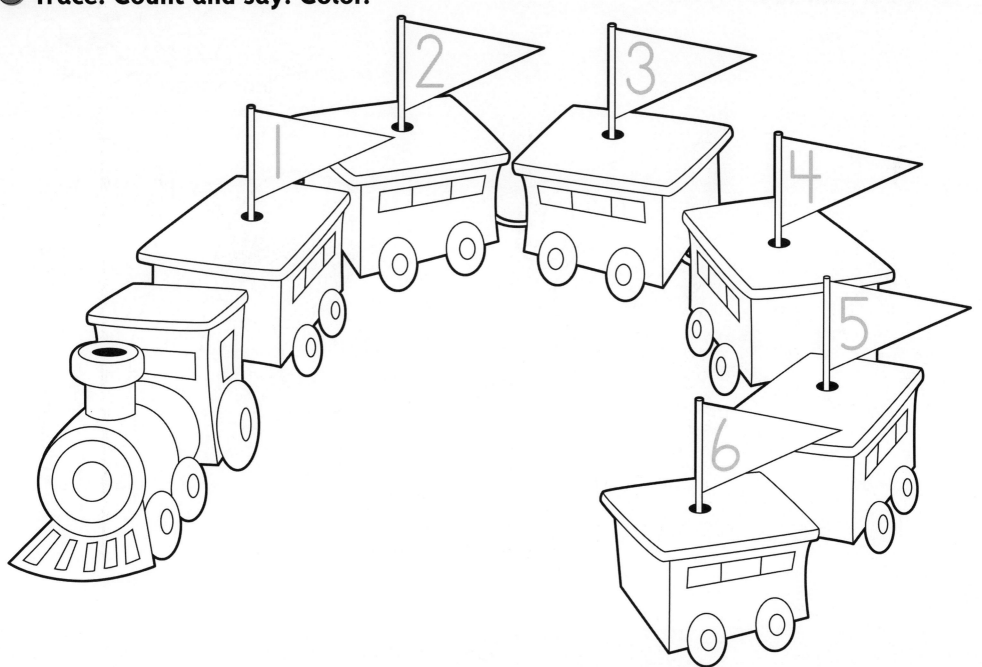

Practice: numbers 1–6, train

VALUES

7 Color and say.

Please share.

Values: Please share. **Review:** *ball*

8 Choose your favorite toy. Draw. Color and say.

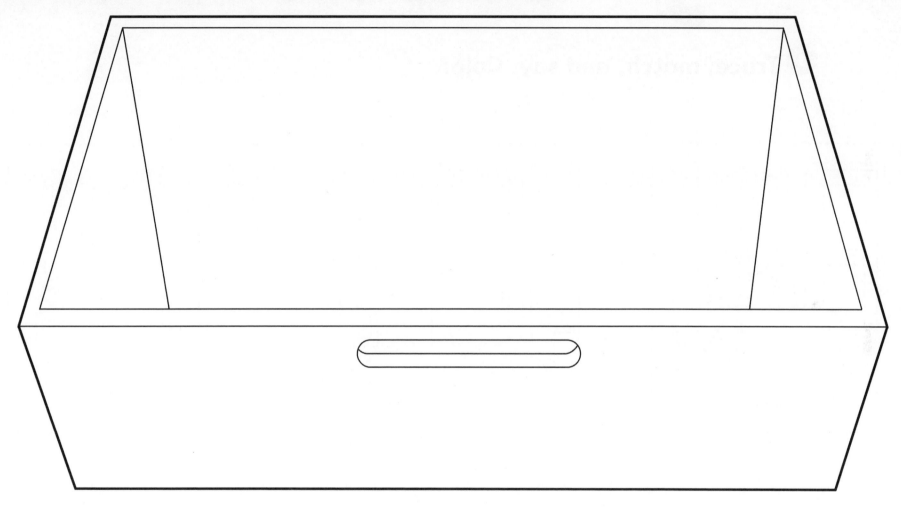

Review: *Is it a [car]? Yes, it is. / No, it isn't.*

5 My House

1 Trace, match, and say. Color.

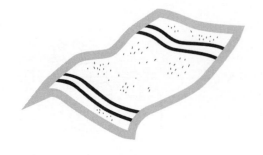  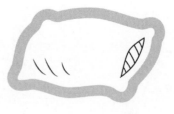

Practice: *bathroom, bedroom, house, kitchen*

2 Where's the dog? Ask and answer. Color.

Practice: *Where's the [dog]? [He's] in the [living room].*

Draw and say. Color.

Where's the duck?

Practice: *Where's the [duck]? It's in the [bathroom].*

SPEAKING

4 **Where's the bike? Ask and answer. Color.**

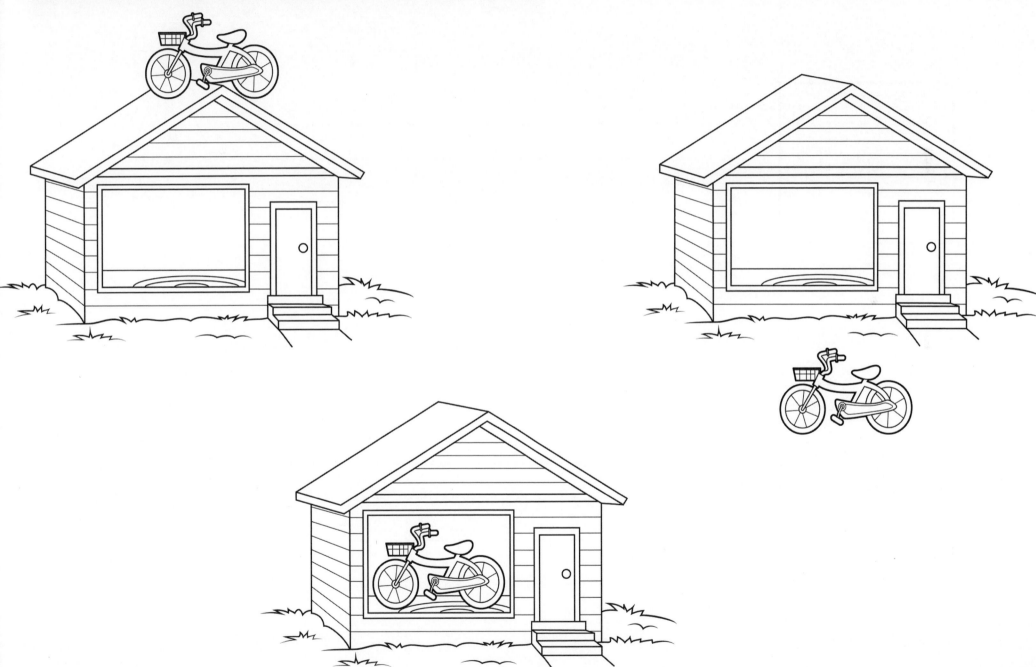

Practice: *Where's the [bike]? It's [in] the house.*

5 Trace, color, and say.

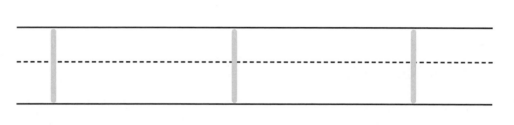

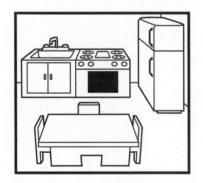

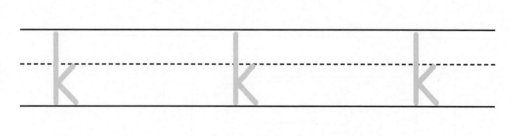

Phonics: initial *l* and *k* sounds **Review:** *kite, lamp*

MATH

6 Find, count, and circle. Color.

1 2 3 4

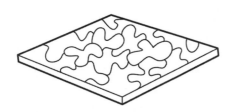
(1) 2 3 4

1 2 3 4

1 2 3 4

1 2 3 4

Practice: numbers 1–4

VALUES

7 **Are they careful? Color and say.**

Be careful!

Values: Be careful.

I can!

8 **Draw your bedroom. Color and say.**

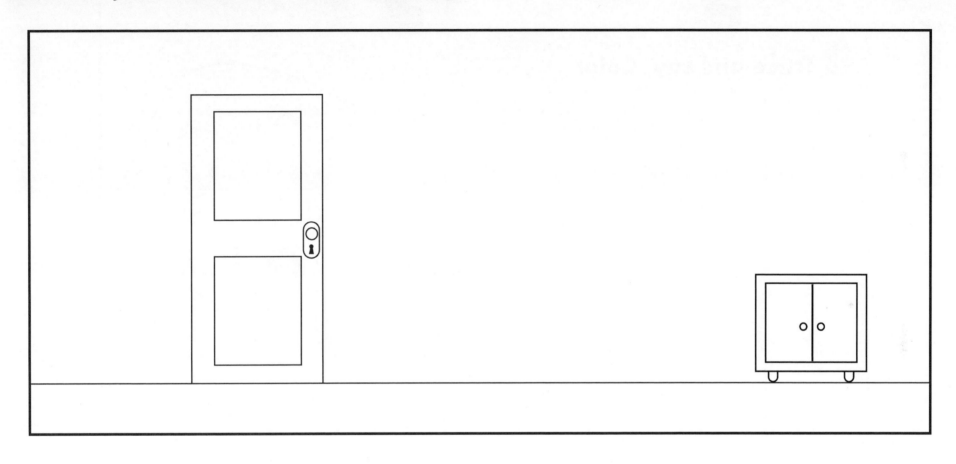

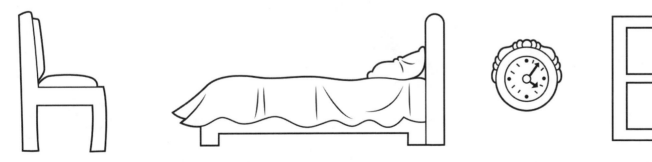

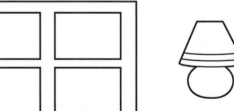

Review: *bedroom; Where's the [chair]? It's in the [bedroom].*

6 My Body

Practice: *arms, body, feet, hands, head, legs*

2 Finish the picture. Color and say.

Practice: *Where's the [head]? This is the [head].*

3 **Circle what's different in Box B. Color and say.**

A   B

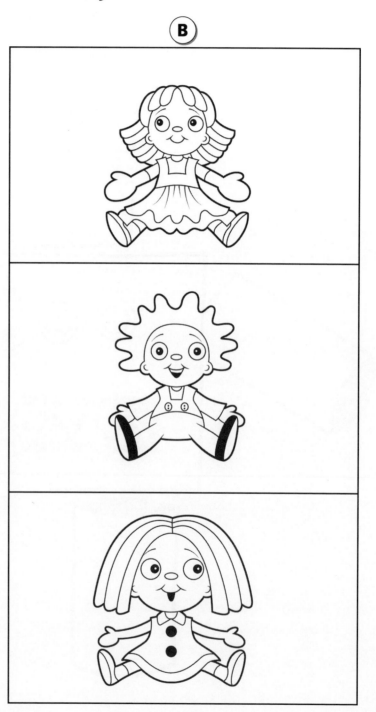

Practice: *These are the [hands]. This is the [head].*

SPEAKING

4 Color and check ☑.

Practice: *These are the [legs].*

Trace, color, and say.

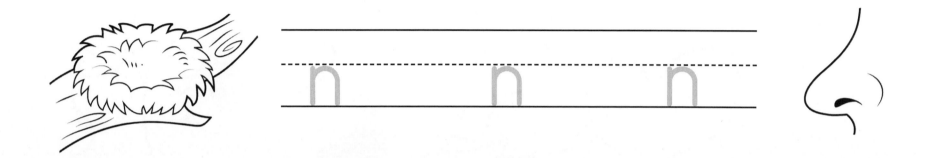

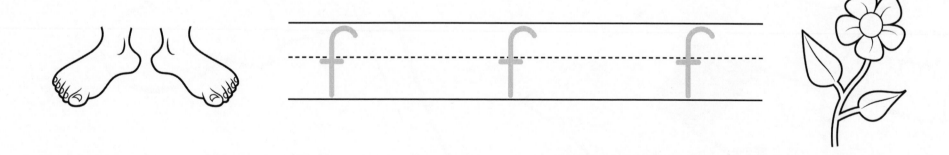

Phonics: initial *n* and *f* sounds **Review:** *nest, nose, flower*

MATH

6 **Count the body parts. Circle the number. Color.**

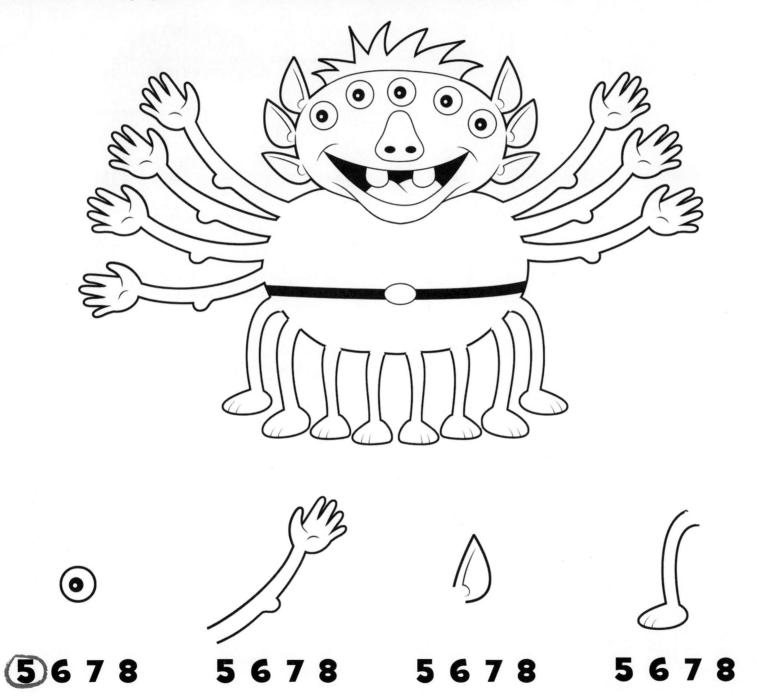

(**5**) 6 7 8   5 6 7 8   5 6 7 8   5 6 7 8

Practice: numbers 5–8; *How many [feet]?*

7 **Who is right? Circle and say. Color.**

Values: Wash your hands.

REVIEW I can!

8 **Draw yourself. Color and say.**

Review: *This is my [head]. These are my [hands].*

7 Time to Eat!

1 Color and say.

Practice: *bread, chicken, cookies, pasta, salad*

STORY

2 **What does Billy like? Circle and color.**

Practice: *Do you like [apples]? Yes, I do. / No, I don't.*

SPEAKING

3 **Ask and answer. Circle or cross out. Color.**

Practice: *Do you like [cake]? Yes, I do. / No, I don't.*

4 **Ask and answer. Draw. Color.**

Do you like bread?

Practice: *Do you like [bread]? Yes, I do. / No, I don't.*

5 Trace, color, and say.

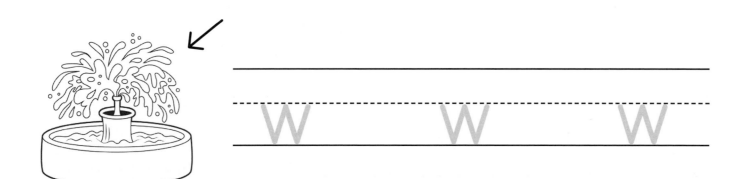

WHITE

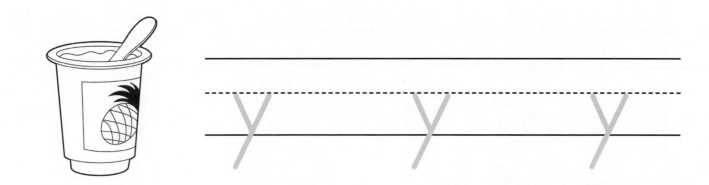

Phonics: initial *w* and *y* sounds **Review:** *water, yogurt*

6 Trace. Count and match. Color.

7   8   9

VALUES

7 **Color and say.**

Eat properly!

Values: Eat properly.

REVIEW — I can!

8 Draw your favorite food. Color and say.

Review: food vocabulary; *Do you like [salad]? Yes, I do. / No, I don't.*

8 On the Farm

1 Circle the different animals. Color and say.

Practice: *cow, duck, goat, hen, horse, sheep*

STORY

2 **Circle the differences in Picture B. Say. Color.**

Ⓐ

Ⓑ

Practice: *Can you see the [duck]? Yes, I can. / No, I can't.*

SPEAKING

3 **Ask and answer. Check ☑ what you see. Color.**

Can you see
the duck?

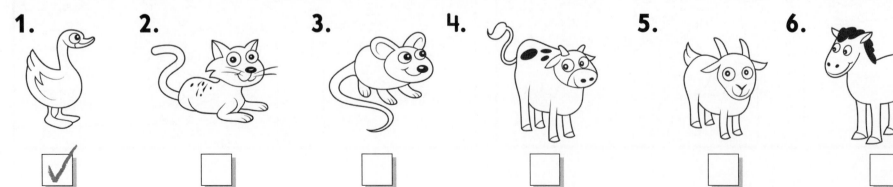

1. ✓   2. ☐   3. ☐   4. ☐   5. ☐   6. ☐

Practice: *Can you see the [duck]? Yes, I can. / No, I can't.*

SPEAKING

4 **What animals can you see? Ask and answer. Color.**

1.

2.

3.

4.

5.

6.

Can you see a cow?

Practice: *Can you see a [cow]? Yes, I can. / No, I can't.*

5 Trace, color, and say.

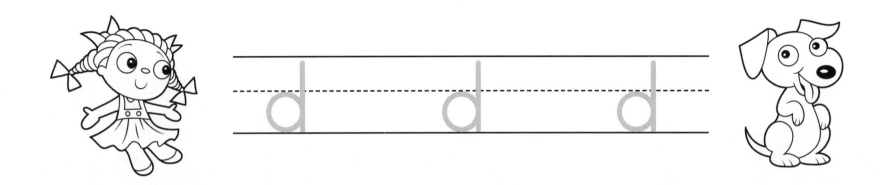

d   d   d

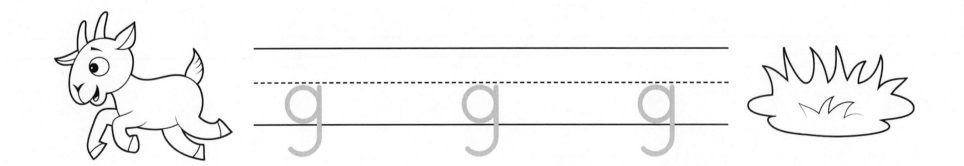

g   g   g

Phonics: initial *d* and *g* sounds **Review:** *dog, doll, grass*

6 **How many? Count and circle. Color.**

8 9 10   **8 9 10**   **8 9 10**

VALUES

7 **Color and say.**

Do your chores.

Values: Do your chores.

I can!

8 Draw your favorite animals. Color and say.

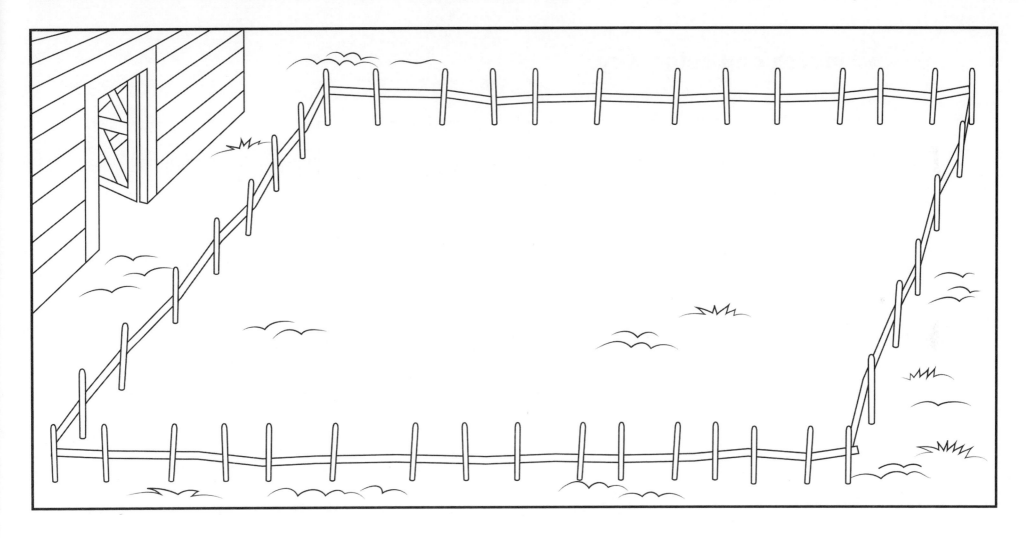

Review: animals; *Can you see a [horse]? Yes, I can. / No, I can't.*

9 The Weather

1 Match and color. Say.

Practice: *cold, hot, rainy, snowy, sunny, windy*

2 **Put the pictures in order. Write 1, 2, 3, and 4.**

___

___

1

___

Practice: *How's the weather? It's [windy].*

3 Spin a pencil. Ask and answer. Color.

Practice: *How's the weather? It's [cold].*

4 **Color and say.**

Practice: *How's the weather? It's [rainy] [snowy] [sunny].*

5 **Trace and match. Color.**

b   d   g   k   l   p   t

Phonics: initial sounds *b, d, g, k, l, p,* and *t* **Review:** *kite, lamp, tree*

6 Trace. Count the shapes and match. Color.

VALUES

7 **Circle the clothes Billy needs. Color and say.**

Dress for the weather.

Values: Dress for the weather.

8 Draw your favorite weather. Color and say.

Review: *How's the weather? It's [sunny].*

LETTER PRACTICE

Find, circle, and say. Color.

Practice: *b, d, t, w*

LETTER PRACTICE

Find, circle, and say. Color.

LETTER PRACTICE

Find, circle, and say. Color.

Practice: *f, g, k, l*

WORD PRACTICE

Trace and say. Color.

bike

goat

duck

kite

fish

lamp

WORD PRACTICE

Trace and say. Color.

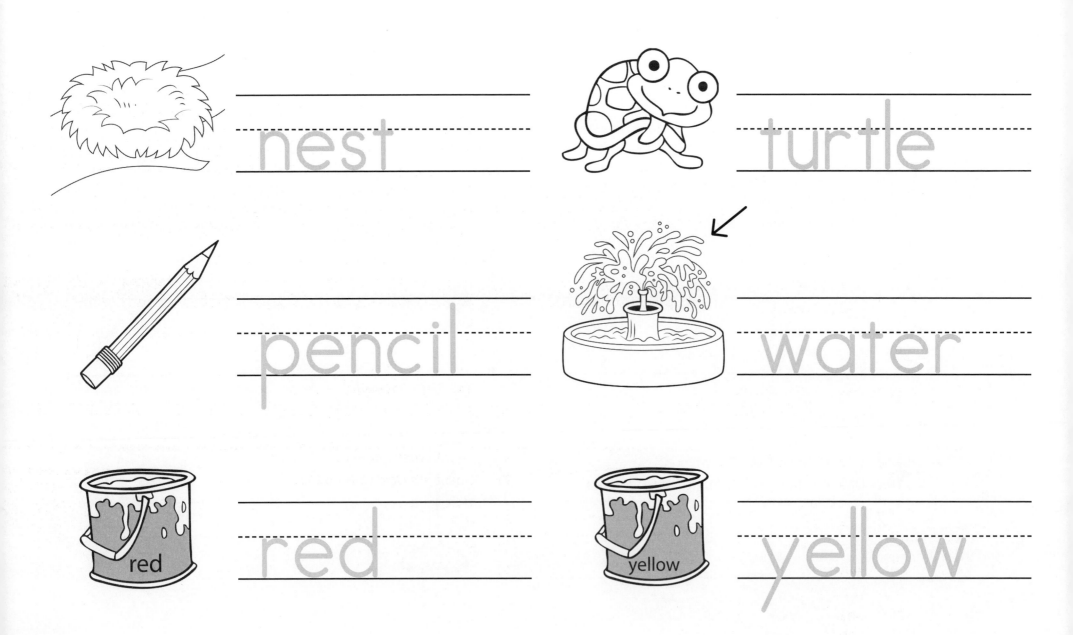

nest

turtle

pencil

water

red

yellow

Practice: *nest, pencil, red, turtle, water, yellow*